THE FIRST HAY(NA)KU ANTHOLOGY

Edited By

JEAN VENGUA & MARK YOUNG

Meritage Press
USA

xPress(ed)
Finland

2005

This selection Copyright ©2005 by the Editors.
Individual pieces Copyright ©2005 by their respective authors.

All rights reserved. No part of this book may be reproduced in any form or by any means, electronic or mechanical, including printing, photocopying, recording, or by any information storage or retrieval system, without permission in writing from the publishers.

FIRST EDITION

Design & Typesetting
by Mark Young & Jukka-Pekka Kervinen

Cover art by Jukka-Pekka Kervinen
Copyright ©2005
.

Co-published by
Meritage Press
St. Helena & San Francisco, CA
http://www.meritagepress.com

&

xPress(ed)
Espoo, Finland
http://www.xpressed.org

Printed in USA

Vengua, Jean and Young, Mark
The First Hay(na)ku Anthology / Vengua, Jean and Young, Mark . — 1st ed.
Poetry. Essays on poetics. Multiculural studies. Creative writing.
ISBN 951-9198-72-5

ACKNOWLEDGEMENTS

Some of these poems have previously appeared on the following weblogs: A New Broom, As/Is, Crag Hill's Poetry Scorecard, hay(na)ku, gasps, jgarverhaynaku, Makura-no-soshi, Marsh Hawk Press, Muisti|kirja, Negative Wingspan, Ruby Street, Stamen Pistol, The Chatelaine's Poetics & Vanishing Points of Resemblance / Unprotected Texts.

Thomas Fink's **Hay(na)ku Sequence 3** is a revision of **(Un)tenured Tsunami**, included in *Gossip*, Marsh Hawk Press, 2001.

Kirsten Kaschock's **Sunday Number Theory** was published in Eileen Tabios' book *I Take Thee, English, for My Beloved*, Marsh Hawk Press, 2004.

Sandy McIntosh's **My Hay(na)ku** was first published in his *The After-Death History of My Mother*, Marsh Hawk Press, 2005.

Radhey Shiam's **rumour** was first published in the periodical *Bhavan's Journal*. Our thanks to the editor.

For Nico Vassilakis, Quarrying About Hay(na)ku was originally posted to Crag Hill's Poetry Scorecard.

An earlier version of Eileen Tabios' essay appeared in *I Take Thee, English, for My Beloved*, Marsh Hawk Press, 2004.

The lines used by harry k. stammer are from **SELF-PORTRAIT IN A CONVEX MIRROR** by John Ashbery, copyright © 1972, 1973, 1974, 1975 by John Ashbery. Used by permission of Viking Penguin, a division of Penguin Group (U.S.A.) Inc.

The editors would like to thank Catalina Cariaga and Luisa Igloria for their generosity in providing information for Jean Vengua's essay.

The composition on the cover by Jukka-Pekka Kervinen is based on a Mark Young hay(na)ku "The / clouds have / been replaced by // a / smoke haze / on the horizon."

CONTENTS

A not so tercet note	Mark Young	6
The Chicken and The Egg	Jean Vengua	7
For Nico Vassilakis,		
Quarrying about Hay(na)ku	Crag Hill	8
One year after it began	The Editors	9

The Hay(na)ku

Ivy Alvarez	11
Tom Beckett	12
Tom Beckett, Eileen Tabios & Mark Young	16
Raymond Calbay	17
Michael Chmielecki	18
Nicholas Downing	19
Jilly Dybka	24
Monica Fauble	25
Thomas Fink	27
Thomas & Maya Mason Fink	28
Craig Freeman	29
Michael Helsem	32
Crag Hill	33
Jill Jones	40
Kirsten Kaschock	44
Rachael Kendrick	47
Karri Kokko	49
Tucker Leiberman	50
Andrew Lundwall	50
Sandy McIntosh	52
Sheila E. Murphy	53
David Nemeth	56
Aimee Nezhukumatathil	57
Shin Yu Pai	58
Vincent Ponka	58
Ernesto Priego	58

Francis Raven	63
Barbara Jane Reyes	65
Jay Rosevear	68
Jim Ryals	69
Radhey Shiam	69
harry k. stammer	70
Eileen Tabios	71
Jean Vengua, harry k. stammer & Mark Young	71
Jean Vengua	72
Dan Waber	73
David C. Whiteman	73
Tanya Williamson	74
James A. Wren	74
Mark Young	75
---	---	---
The History of the Hay(na)ku	Eileen Tabios	77

Notes on the Hay(na)ku from Contributors	86
Notes on the Editors	90
Notes on Contributors	91

A not so tercet note
- Mark Young

It's almost paradoxical to be writing an essay about hay(na)ku, a form that's extremely simple & has few rules – "Six / words. Three / lines. One poem." But don't let the simplicity deceive. It's simple in the sense that a wormhole that passes through the space/time continuum is simple, &, what's more, you're not expected to know the physics of it.

The creation myth of the form has the serendipity associated with all great discoveries, the right person in the right place at the right time able to transmute the conjunction of a number of things to produce something that goes beyond them all – a quote from a Kerouac letter exposing itself as it fell from an elegant knee, Brautigan counting in the background of the mind, a cultural heritage of sufficient elasticity to be able to absorb the form, taste it & say "Haynaku! This is as easy as one-two-three."

& then there's the similarity in name to the Japanese haiku. Plus a similar structure. But hay(na)ku is an exception to the quacking duck analogy. Haiku are hidebound with restrictions – seasonal cyphers, seventeen syllables, the proscription on more than one strophe unless you're writing with someone else, bouncing verses back & forth like one of Corso's poets hitchhiking on the highway. & then there's the *Aha-Erlebnis*, the Aha!-experience, that's almost mandatory for the final line.

Hay(na)ku are open. Any subject. No code. Words can be as short or as long as you want them to be. There can be any number of verses. The usual 1/2/3 form is expansionary both to the writer & the reader. To quote Crag Hill from his piece a few pages on:

> I've been attracted by the line I've seen in these poems: limber, bending, stretching, a yoga, something I haven't felt much in the poetics of the line in poetry of the last twenty years. These lines have hinges, armature, as well as full-ranging shoulders and hips.

Hay(na)ku is officially defined as a diasporic poetic. Eileen Tabios, in her essay on the history of the hay(na)ku that accompanies this, refers to the diaspora of the Filipinos, how there are eight million of them scattered around the globe. New Zealanders, too, are diasporic. There is a standing joke that could the last New Zealander to leave the country please turn out the lights. & poets too, by nature & craft, have embarked on their own diaspora even if they never leave home.

Regard hay(na)ku then as postcards from wherever their author has touched earth. They can depict something as simple as a cormorant sitting on a bollard or as complex as any painting by Hieronymous Bosch. To close with one of my own:

> Hay(na)ku
> are both
> seed & tree.

§

The Chicken and the Egg
- Jean Vengua

While we may acknowledge the Japanese haiku's traditional focus on brevity, the tercet form called "hay(na)ku" is even more brief; it springs from the space and breath of an exclamation. The term in its common Filipino usage registers a moment of excess, a brief venting of some interior emotion: "Hay, nakú!" The "hay" part (pronounced like a long "I") is an exclamation similar to "Oh!", "Ay!", or "Oy!" According to the *Tagalog-English Dictionary* edited by Leo James English, C.Ss.R., "nakú" comes from the term, Iná (mother) ko! (my), or "my mother!" In fact, the pronoun, "ku" is pronounced more like "ko". The synonym given in the Dictionary is "Madre mía!" in Spanish.

On the other hand, there is the egg, or offspring theory. Catalina Cariaga argues that the term, hay, nakú, comes from the Ilocano word for child, "anák". Her mother would exclaim, "Hay, anák-o!" (Ay, my child!). Luisa Igloria remembers that "the Ilocano phrases equivalent to "m'ijo" or "m'ija" (Spanish), were indeed "anak co". Compact, but containing infinite potential, the egg can crack open and become many, maanák. In a brief phrase, one can express surprise, dismay, shock, or register a mild curse. Cariaga recalls that, as an errant child, hearing that phrase could also mean that she was "busted." She insists that "hay, nakú!" is a term used familiarly; that you are more likely to use it around family and friends than to use it around strangers.

Ernesto Priego writes: "I feel the hay(na)ku is a form that grants a common space for poetic practice in different languages; a way of writing in English without completely obliterating one's "mothertongue". In an e-mail message to me, Luisa Igloria notes that "…the word "naku" occurs in other Southeast Asian languages and dialects, including Japanese, Indian, Polynesian, not to mention in some Latin American indigenous cultures". There are over one hundred seventy languages in the Philippine archipelago, and no doubt, all of them have their own way of expressing "hay nakú!"

My point is not to claim a precise etymology, or to worry about which came first (chicken or egg), but maybe just to note that, despite its brevity, the name of the form contains precious memory, especially in those two letters contained like a yolk in parentheses; it is both "mothertongue" and "offspring", even as it pays tribute to the Japanese haiku, which happens to play itself out in more formal refrains. I first encountered the hay(na)ku on the internet. In this medium, it has passed around quickly, globally; poet-bloggers have tried it, nursed it, tasted and tested it. I suppose that poets will each perceive it through the lens of their own locale and language. The hay(na)ku remembers what it is: a product of diaspora, its seeds scatter, searching for good ground.

§

For Nico Vassilakis, Quarrying About Hay(na)ku:
- Crag Hill

> ("crag, curious about these here hay/na/ku's i looked around for definite descript but it seems it's just one two two three three three is that right? is there another constraint involved? subject? length? mood? syllabic? is it a blog product? or something that quivers herein unchecked?")

Nico, as far as I can tell, the two primary criteria of an hay(na)ku poem are tercets comprised of a one word line, followed by a two word line, capped by a three word line.

A blog product? The form first caught my eye on the As/Is blog, especially the hay(na)ku produced by Mark Young and Tom Beckett. These poems had the immediacy of haiku with more, much more surface and sub-surface/versive potential. Word count shapes the line, not a syllabic, accentual, parsing (though I think hay(na)ku is open to a variation that could include a tercet made up of a one-syllable line, followed by a two syllable line, underlined by a three syllable line). I've been attracted by the line I've seen in these poems: limber, bending, stretching, a yoga, something I haven't felt much in the poetics of the line in poetry of the last twenty years. These lines have hinges, armature, as well as full-ranging shoulders and hips. Check some of Mark Young's poems out on As/Is and **pelican dreaming**. They've got a dance I've found quite appealing of late.

I'm not sure when Eileen Tabios birthed this form, but it's grown exponentially. Although it must not be more than a year old, there's an anthology in the works. I'll paste in the submissions call which provides some more information.

§

One year after it began
- Jean Vengua & Mark Young

During the course of the toing and froing between editors and authors that comes with putting an anthology together, Tom Beckett remarked in an email that "an equally terrific anthology could have been put together using entirely different poems." And that's true, for a couple of reasons.

The first is based on space. We wanted to include as wide a range of poets as possible, so that meant leaving out equally-deserving poems from some of those to whom we'd already given broad representation.

The second factor is time. This anthology had a close-off date for submissions, and so, when we sifted through the poems that had already been published elsewhere, we also used this date. Certainly a couple of late additions snuck in under the wire; but if we'd left it open, selecting a finite anthology would have been a Sisyphian task since so much good work is continuing to appear.

Tom Beckett has written what may well be considered the first hay(na)ku "classic", his *Wittgenstein Études*, a series of 27 three-verse poems. Crag Hill, Sheila E. Murphy, Ernesto Priego and Jill Jones continue to use the form as an integral part of their poetry. More poets have started writing hay(na)ku; established – e.g. Lorna Dee Cervantes - and not so established – e.g. Scott Glassman and Rebeka Lembo. Hay(na)ku have moved out of the blogs & into collections. And Eileen Tabios has disproved once and for all her claim that she is "mediocre at the form" with her recent sequence *The Hay(na)ku of Numbers*.

So, as the hay(na)ku continues to spread, to grow, to develop, we offer this anthology as an interim summary, not a conclusion.

IVY ALVAREZ

'What are poets for in a destitute time?'
—Friedrich Hölderlin

Poets
are good
to eat, as

they
are more
tender and juicy

than
any other
human. Any cannibal

worth
his/her
salt knows this.

TOM BECKETT

Language
is the
fabric of consciousness.

The
responsibility of
poets? To attend

to
its woof
and weave -- to

unravel
it, even.
Paying close attention

is,
in itself,
a political act.

Dear Reader,

I
am speaking.
To you. Now.

This
or that
has happened. Again.

You
and I
should get together.

Maybe
we will
fall in love.

Stammered Hay(na)ku

Only
an erasing
hand can write

can
right the
list of love

§

To
hurt oneself
learning to feel

what
one has
not felt before.

To
hurt oneself
refusing to feel

what
one once
before had felt.

Why Does Poetry Matter?

It
is a
part of reality

that
once apprehended
can change reality.

§

I
think that
kissing is perhaps

one
of the
most important things

that
we fragile
human beings do.

Think
about how
you do it.

§

I
dance badly
but I dance.

I
sing poorly
but I sing.

Kiss
me. I
am a poet.

§

Breaking
the plane
of another's surface.

§

One
and one
are not two

Curse you, hay(na)ku. You are the mistress I cannot leave.

It
will leak
out into likelihood.

It
will lick
at the edges

of
the boundaries
of perception. It

will
look *out*.
It will transpire

in
series of
sentences idealized in

screens
drawn against
the empirical world.

TOM BECKETT, EILEEN TABIOS & MARK YOUNG

Night

At
night the
landscape is anonymous.

At
night the
landscape is autonomous.

Night
is landscape
Walk with me

Night
is language.
And I will.

Night
is linkage.
What of you?

Hand
in hand —
the night harmonious!

RAYMOND CALBAY

In
my palms,
a maya sings

as
my soles
sprout roots digging

deep,
chasing the
trail of rain.

MICHAEL CHMIELECKI

Morning paper

What
is a
word that begins

with
end? A
word that wanders

within
morning papers --
unfolding pages. Silence,

our
silence, balanced
on white opals.

Soliloquy

Hammers
wear velvet
in certain sounds.

NICHOLAS DOWNING

because

my neighbor wants
me dead
because

i have beautiful
hair my
mother

beat me because
she loved
me

she told me
in the
old

country her father
would kill
men

with a machete
because they
looked

at her mother
she was
beautiful

like me and
beauty makes
men

do strange things
she told
me

we need protection
from evil
and

from men who
cannot control
themselves

tomorrow will not
be different
because

nothing changes i'm
so stupid
beauty

makes me vulnerable
it's my
fate

to be a
slave to
it

my mother tells
me i
suffer

because i'm not
plain like
her

this makes sense
my mother's
strong

she can hide
from evil
but

i can't i
try i
really

try but i
see my
neighbor

watching me story
of my
life

§

a rusted spiral
discolored pale
sunset

long net casting
shadows she
is

practicing the a-scale
on the
patio

pine trees sway
beneath the
lightning

sky brighter than
sun sun darker
than

sky sometimes I'm
even someone
else

§

or
call it
a snake, profligate

and
spitting, commuters
running after it.

§

bikini among prosody
three words
that

if
you repeat
often enough cease

to mean absolutely
anything at
all

§

we
are bound
by the mind

we
are bound
by its function

until
we widen
into its body

§

what
i'm trying
to tell you

is
that i'm
trying to tell

you
i am
trying yes you

say
with a
smile very trying.

JILLY DYBKA

Mega,
giga. Not
far enough away.

§

Facing
this way
and that. Cows.

MONICA FAUBLE

Dawn

Open
window like
a lit match

Morning Routine

Walking
the wrap
of the river.

Form

My skirts shorter
than these
lines.

Torn, Teeth, Tearing

I'd
like to
say I understand

about
loss, but
what does it

mean
to rip
meat from the

bone?

Arriving Home Eager After Modern-Dance Class

The only option
is to
roll

cross-lateral across the
length of
my

one-room apartment. Flooring
not designed
for

this, my spine
forms knots
and

handles. My body
full of
breathe

and heat, my
back blistered
by

windows and doors.
Grip tight.
Pull

hard.

THOMAS FINK

from: Hay(na)ku box sequence 2

You,
collecting pockets,
can one spiral
into
an honest
magnet? I have
fished
thrift. We
await them impatiently.

Haynaku Sequence 3

Article
that none
drank, but backlash

quails
hegemony, lottery
to grief. Your

instructor
will define
you for seven

weeks.
A solid
we. Round up

the
undecidables for
dinner, Junior. Be

lovely,
erase offending
error spawn. Spaghetti

detained
for impersonating
lo mein. Will

ramen
be testifying
for the defense?

THOMAS & MAYA MASON FINK

Earliest Memory Haynaku

I
was crawling
up the tempting

steps.
Dad was
yapping on the

painted
phone. My
curly sister summoned

him
to ungently
shuffle me down.

CRAIG FREEMAN

clear
also blemish
edge of other
program
branch nut
 rhythm of tail
genus
 pitches heart
as the weight
to sorts
to load again
pugs

Even
The impression
Does not fit

But
By what
A mode proceeds

As
Ourself fits
Rather than others

As
Under the
Influence of stars

§

breaks
a string
that dead dragon

it
was when
the grasshoppers gave

praise
of the
serpent through dirge

§

Moonshine
And great
Quantities of hills

§

demons
love men
in such ways

as
to bring
them to fire

unquenchable

MICHAEL HELSEM

"A Shadow Over Westchester"

words
are born
free, yet everywhere

the
only emperor
is the emperor

gray
clouds march
across the ruins

gods,
feared, whatever
they might be

§

new
habits, the
glue still wet

CRAG HILL

Rewriting a Proposition from Camus

Judging
whether life
is or is

not
worth loving
amounts to swerving

around
the elemental
quest of perspective

Highway to Hill

more
snow than
knowing, and though

the
layers insulate
dormant winter wheat

roads
slip, spin
an unintended swerve

a
straight line
discovers its driver

my
place is
not a ditch

On the Wall

I
could ask
you about yourself

period
or I
could ask you

how
you live
how you love

or
if honest
I could ask

myself
these questions
then ask you

how
we co-exist
especially considering I

am
the one
doing the talking

overheard

and
you know,
Dad, I can

see
that some
women do indeed

look
a little
like acoustic guitars

Spring's Sprung
for Tom, Eileen, Stephen Stills, and Norman's brother

if
the garden
is the earth's

bellybutton
as Liam
and Noemi say

then
her genitals
must be near

omnipresent
omniscient, in
constant low level-stimulation

so
earth spins
as earthquakes rock

so
mountains build
to precipitous climax

Testing the Watering

Which
comes first
the fist growing

inward
or thirst
imploding, the test

of
the word
flooding out itself?

She
stands kneedeep,
her silence flowing,

in
expert knowledge
of her limitations

when
she plunges
out of sight

drowning
the undeniable
taste of depth

I Know Now

it
turns somewhere
seems to taunt

turns
out of
knowing, burns, spits

before
it spins
off into needing

absolutely
nothing in
the dumb center

Or On

some
dominant terrain
that wrangle of

harm
and gel,
size and sweet

weather
periscoped through
my boardroom keepsake

…what
turned out
my inset cries

Heaving Seas

yet
what eyes
I haunted, why

I
shelled half
my laugh response

sneezed
aside a
sand conduit when

I
can comb
mean and loosen

a
pace in
my own choir

Press Corpse Question

in
that space
behind your eyes

your
hollow words
echoing, how large

are
you really?
large enough to

know
how truly
small you are?

Cultivating Seasons

in
the summer
of my life

weeding
the crops
pruning overgrown branches

watering
the vines
of my brain

tending
the garden
that will feed

my
inevitable winter
I've this urge

to
dig new
ground even if

no
harvest ever
comes from it

JILL JONES

impermanent tenses 1

many
ways to
talk through pulp

glass
the skin
mistakes of language

talking
within each
other in pursuit

our
own best
and holy season

still
singing in
the gloaming gut

and
hung beating
rhythm the reflection

I
give up
in the stroke

the
body fails
even its excuses

I
watch myself
lost inside myself

self's
changing ratio
letterbox pan widescreen

hear
little stings
from phones redundant

testing
situation with
the real/ word

life
takes place
on planets sleek

smoky
we travel
our uncertain seats

cheeky
corners render
moments of disappearance

impermanent tenses 2

our
staggering stuff
in nested containers

excess
looking back
while going forward

silent
or sung
too little being

graffiti
creaking rail
the hissing pneumos

volcanoes
sound lava
from old women

cradled
in their
mouths and lyrics

quilts
culture above
the minimalist abyss

voices
dolcissimo marzipan
a little more

dreamt
of original
bliss letting the

pleasure
go 'way
out' signs past

Wet waiting arms

Hands
of the
full tide drift

mist
the river
oars long sighs

lizard
sun wall
shadow, not you

chorus
white blossom
steps of rain

notes
next door
fret down channel

waking
useless empty
kiss of morning

scuffles
in branches
magpie jealous nest

jasmine
risen fences
night cool nostalgia

forgotten
skin touch
purple night flower

tracing
the hill
draw in breath

KIRSTEN KASCHOCK

I am saving it

For
The rain —
My other virginity

Sunday Number Theory

One
is consummate.
One is mouth

navel
and anus
— a clear digestive

loop.
One is
broth. Is consommé.

One's
flavor is
salt. One exists

by
the narrowest
margin. One has

this
one-word motto:
stay. One cannot

regroup.
Once split,
one has broken

every
oath — which
was the one

oath —
to be
bound as one

eternally.
So — orphan.
One cannot be

named
nor be
known. One is

god —
worshipless. Shamed
by god's need:

worship.
One's sound
is one tree

splitting
the head
of an angel

— then
the tree
must burn, angel

burn,
and pins
trace hymns through

soot.
One stops
at nothing: train

beyond
breaking — point
forfeit to motion.

One
has no
equivalent, no

one
in which
to trust, no

one
to marry,
no other one

to
bed. All
said is also

done.
It is
a fearful promise —

one.

RACHAEL KENDRICK

step
one then
down again

this
is me
starting again, tom

I
can only
do it if

it's
a conversation
I can when you're

in
the room
what kind of

dependence
is this
when it's not

my
voice that's
still but my

eternally
restless hands
always pecking searching

staring
looking for
something better to

feed.

i'm

getting

un foc
used

§

better
walk as
the earth guides.

better
let these
knees walk alone.

if
not now
then where to?

if
not you
then with who?

KARRI KOKKO

Tänä
yönä sinun
nimesi imi lumi.

A note on the poem above.

The literal translation would be "Tonight your name was sucked up (or absorbed) by snow" but I dare not try to work that into a hay(na)ku because so much would be missing. For one, in the Finnish original, the first two lines could also be understood as "Tonight I'm yours." And the last line is pure sound play: nimesi = your name, imi = sucked up (by), lumi = snow. The nominative, not the genitive, form of "name" would be even better: nimi. Think about it: nimi imi lumi (with all the i's pronounced as very short e's). The whole thing started the other night when I was staring at the snow outside my window. There were no sounds because the snow works as a muffler. It's very eerie, and soothing. (There, we already got two words – snow and soothing.)

p.s. (Hay(na)ku) when pronounced means "July" (heinäkuu) in Finnish.

TUCKER LEIBERMAN

OSNext

each
operating system
brings new life

OS25
platform of
seed and rebellion

OS50
midlife crisis
hot flashing frozen

OS75
swings and
reboots in style

home
release again
into open source

ANDREW LUNDWALL

partial list #1

sunshine
dada lemonade
my manic preoccupation

partial list #2

porcupine
soft felt
red light district

§

listening
to nico
"eulogy to lenny

bruce"
wondering why
i am still

alive
the first
day chased by

the
last day
taps me on

the
shoulder need
addicted to loss

the
equation always
moves onwards me

SANDY McINTOSH

My Hay(Na)Ku
(With Handy Pronunciation Guide for Public Performance)

Lorca!
His foot
in the doorway!

Pronunciation Guide:

 "L" as second "l" in "Llewellyn"
"o" as "o" in "amoeba"
"r" as "r" in Southern US pronunciation of "cornpone"
"c" as fourth "c" in "acciaccatura"
"a" as "a" in "aesthetic"
"H" as "h" in "catachresis"
"i" as "i" in "poiesis"
"s" as second "s" in "sans serif"
"f" as first "f" in "afflatus"
"o" as second "o" in alternate spelling "encyclopoedia"
"o" as second "o" in alternate spelling "encyclopoedia"
"t" as first "t" in "attorney"
"i" as "i" in "poiesis"
"n" as "n" in "limn"
"t" as first "t" in "attorney"
"h" as "h" in "catachresis"
"e" as "e" in "eidetic"
"d" as first "d" in "addiction"
"o" as second "o" in alternate spelling "encyclopoedia"
"o" as second "o" in alternate spelling "encyclopoedia"
"r" as "r" in Southern US pronunciation of "cornpone"
"w" as "w" in "wrist"
"a" as "a" in "aesthetic"

NOTE: "Y" is pronounced "the the".

SHEILA E. MURPHY

Grace

just these eighty-
eight keys
available

*

your tall voice
making light
tones

*

rest is all
about the
notes

*

quiet
unto ample
speech equals sonority

*

pitched
toward flight
such long leaning

*

neighborhood
awash in
ample beatific shadows

Boylight

differently made wings
traverse plush
distances
clouds
erase themselves
reveal muscular blue

§

voyeur
seeking window
Windex in hand

§

footfalls
over footpath
seeming accidental once

§

at first fatherless
ink boils
open

§

depth
extracted from
these several surfaces

§

bright
lotion dress
soft white skin

§

timbre
amber limber
song's light trance

§

seclusion
white frost
on cold glass

§

six
a.m.
toute seule encore

§

here
where now
it is warm

§

firelight
our informal
restitution, private life

DAVID NEMETH

alcohol
crawl, fish
thumb print wet

§

scent
hell shot
nail throttle flag

§

empty
charred action
yell slash celluloid

§

crazed
pine needles
rake and bake

AIMEE NEZHUKUMATATHIL

Flames
of Coca-cola
poured into cups.

§

Campfire
shirts smell
like chocolate meat.

§

Spotted
salamander tail
whipped my wrist.

§

In
moon gardens,
everything white glows.

§

Gossip
can break
tiny bird hearts.

SHIN YU PAI

blepheroplasty

in
the I
of the beholder

VINCENT PONKA

great
mountain wind
came down cool

ERNESTO PRIEGO

Aches
like syllables
lost while traveling

§

(Her
hair looks
from her back)

-She
never notices
I am watching-

I
walk swiftly
like a ghost

Unperceived
unseen, unheard
nothing to you

I
am getting
used to this

Where
are we
now, today, immediately?

Wish
I could
stop writing you

Wish
I could
stop doing this

Even
in threes
you keep appearing.

§

Only
you can
tell me off.

Purple
like a
crushed flying insect.

Red
like roses
dead by water.

White
like hands
untouched by time.

Blue
like eyes
multitudes and scarcity.

Black
like dogs
running together, gasping.

Colors
not seen,
experienced like dreams.

Sólo
tú puedes
enfrentarme, regañarme, criticarme.

Purpúrea,
como un
insecto volador apachurrado.

Roja,
como rosas
muertas en agua.

Blanca,
como manos
por tiempo respetadas.

Azul,
como ojos,
multitudes y carencias.

Negra,
como perros
jadeando, corriendo juntos.

Colores
nunca vistos,
experimentados como sueños.

Sunday

It's
a hunger
like no other:

six
past meridian
watch your watch

isle
moving island
communication failed, again.

history
a series
of failed encounters

he
seeks her
but always fails

she
awaits him
always too late.

It's
hard not
to miss perpetually.

It's
hard, indeed,
not to miss.

§

Hay
nada que
"kus" pueda decir

FRANCIS RAVEN

Eleven Hay(na)ku

Scraping
Your almond
Past my ear

Rolled
Grape leaf
Plump Wisteria heat

Dapple
When I
Wanted a tan

Helplessness
Chimney beam
Porous highway's bubble

Vine
Pokes across
Dirt hair shingle

Book
Fits in
Small of back

If,
It doesn't
Lay flat, then

Stolen
Overgrown wings
Call someone's police

Warmth
Pronouns shrugging
Sautéing coat's essence

Cinema's
Cardinal skip
In car's sleep

Perfection's
Leaf burning
Beside fake smile

BARBARA JANE REYES

True Love hay(na)ku

dapat,
ganito ang
pag-ibig -- tunay, tunay.

§

after bulosan

hey!
if you
want to know

what
we are,
then listen carefully:

cities
teem with
our working masses.

we
sell you
the morning paper;

never
do you
see our faces.

we
wave you
through metal detectors;

your
baggage weighs
our weary shoulders.

your
words, our
fluent tongues speak

as
if they
were our own.

your
wars, our
men have fought

as
if they
were our own.

your
land, our
elders have tilled

as
if it
were our own.

your
precious children
we have nurtured

as
if they
were our own.

so
if you
want to know

who
we are,
we are your

ghettos,
we are
your teeming cities.

we
are your
darkness, your other.

we
are your
mirror, we are

we
are, we
are, we are…

JAY ROSEVEAR

hedge
fragile white
in an easterly

point
beyond me
and for which

tall
strong outside
as if enough

tinder
touchwood dry
tender would touch

tell
reproach from
making a mark

exhale
pitch block
rage the risk

JIM RYALS

Ecstasy
Echoed off
A tiled hallway

RADHEY SHIAM

proverbs
are ornaments
of lady language

§

child
smiles sweetly
home becomes poetry

§

rumour
a bomber
without a pilot

harry k. stammer

o utofcontext'd (J. A. mirrored'd)

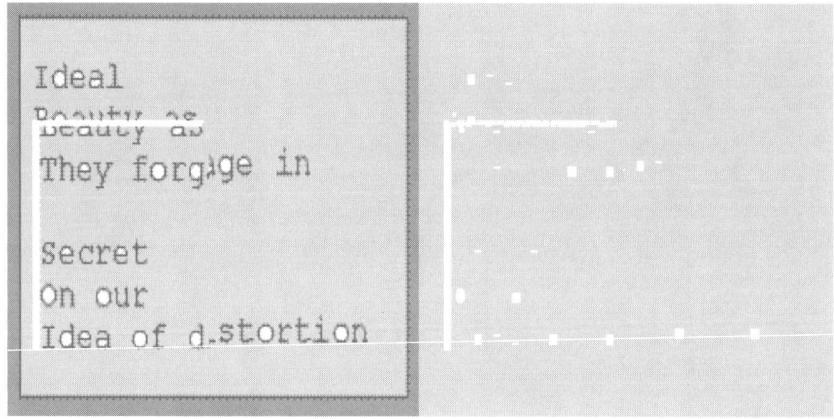

some'ting'other'taine'd

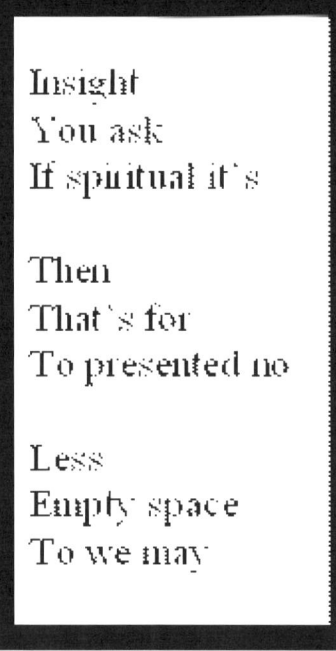

EILEEN TABIOS

Labor Day

gravity
blackens wings
with joyful scars

JEAN VENGUA, harry k. stammer & MARK YOUNG

Ur Burial

burn
we burning
you burning us

§

b
ur
nus

b
ur
new

§

Ur
news. Burnouses
burning. Burn us.

§

Ur
as was
burns as is.

JEAN VENGUA

After Ken Friedman's "Zen is When" (1965)

A placement.
A fragment of time identified.
Brief choreography.

place
"A" identified:
fragment of time

A:
fragment of
brief choreography

brief
fragment identified:
chore of A

a
chore o
a graph o

choreo
graphy a
brief fragment of

frag
of time
of brief placement

place
meant time
brief identity fragment

choreograph
Y place
A and graph

DAN WABER

Spend
more money
on poetry books.

§

Two
triple cheeseburgers,
one diet coke.

§

Nothing
adds up.
Love isn't math.

DAVID C. WHITEMAN

from: Fountain

Fountain
Running water
Fallen pine needles

Feather
Black quill
Floating on surface

Rain
Falling sky
The water stops.

TANYA WILLIAMSON

from: On Breathing

Breathe
as deep
as you dare.

JAMES A. WREN

Shots in the Dark #5

already
before me
frozen in time

death
mosquito netting
hung to dry

MARK YOUNG

Ella Fitzgerald in Budapest

Something
I have
always found disappointing,

hearing
a singer
in concert, hearing

a
recording of
that singer some-

where
else, some
years later on.

The
same song,
The Lady is

a
Tramp, music
by straight George,

lyrics
by gay
Ira, Ella Fitzgerald

singing.
The voice
a little harsher

than
I remember
but the phrasing

is
the same.
I sing along.

We
'improvise' together.
In unison. I

know
what notes
will come next.

THE HISTORY OF THE HAY(NA)KU
- Eileen Tabios

In September 2000, I began a "Counting Journal" with the idea that counting would "be just another mechanism for me to understand my days." That journal lasted for only five months because I could maintain its underlying obsession, which was to count everything, for only that long. It was inspired, as this first entry explained on 9/20/2000, by:

> Ianthe Brautigan's *You Can't Catch Death—A Daughter's Memoir* which noted the character Cameron in her father Richard Brautigan's *The Hawkline Monster*: "Cameron was a counter. He vomited nineteen times to San Francisco. He liked to count everything."

A month later, I would write: "I am in library intending to finish reading in one seating Richard Brautigan's *An Unfortunate Woman*. From P. 77:

> "I've always had at times a certain interest in counting. I don't know why this is. It seems to come without a preconceived plan and then my counting goes away. Often without me ever having noticed its departure.
>
> I think I counted the words on the early pages of this book because I wanted to have a feeling of continuity, that I was actually doing something, though I don't know exactly why counting words on a piece of paper served that purpose because I was actually doing something.
>
> Anyway, I stopped counting words on page 22 on February 1, 1982, with a total of 1,885 words. I hope that is the correct sum. I can count, but I can't add which, in itself, is sort of interesting."

Fast forward to June 10, 2003 where I am writing in my first poetics blog, "WINEPOETICS" at http://winepoetics.blogspot.com. On the blog, I'd been excerpting from the Counting Journal.   At this point, I decide to write one last counting-related blog entry, which became:

> But rather than spend more days having you witness me gazing into that part of my navel where Brautigan's eyes are twinkling back, let me write just one last Counting post. This one will feature snippets based on which page the journal opens to when I drop it on the floor. The idea came to me when .... I dropped the journal on the floor as I

was polishing off my 2nd glass of the 2001 Dutch Henry Los Carneros Chardonnay.

Drop Journal: Page opens onto 12/18/00. Bush secured Electoral College majority—271 votes—to become the U.S.' 43rd President. It was announced that Hillary Clinton received an $8.0 mio. advance for a memoir for her years in the White House. W/ Simon and Schuster. So much $ for tsismis, whereas one can't even find $5,000 to publish a poetry book!

Ugh. Close Journal. Drop Journal Again. Page opens onto 1/28/01: On plane returning to San Francisco, read *Selected Letters of Jack Kerouac*. P. 46—Kerouac says, "I think American haikus should never have more than 3 words in a line—e.g.

Trees can't reach
for a glass
of water

I am inaugurating the Filipino Haiku [PinoyPoets: Attention! I'll post if you send me some!]: 3 lines each having one, two, three words in order—e.g.

Trees
can't reach
for a glass

*****

Enough poets responded to my blog-post so that I was able to announce just two days later:

PHILIPPINE INDEPENDENCE DAY ~~ PINOY HAIKU

It seems most apt to introduce the "Pinoy Haiku" on June 12, Philippine Independence Day. This was the day in 1898 that General Emilio Aguinaldo proclaimed Philippine independence from Spain.

But soon afterwards, the United States—having just tasted, and found sweet, its entry as a world power into the arena of global politics—chose not to recognize the Philippines's successfully fought battle for self-determination.

The U.S. invaded the Philippines to turn it into a colony. It wasn't until 1946 that the U.S. formally ended its colonial regime on a day coinciding with the U.S. Independence Day of July 4. Consequently, the Philippines only began to commemorate June 12 in the early 1960s when President Diosdado Macapagal changed Philippine Independence Day from the 4th of July to June 12….

Filipino poets responded to my call for the "Pinoy Haiku" with enthusiasm. Perhaps in part because, as Michelle Bautista pointed out, the idea of one-two-three "works with the Filipino nursery rhyme: *isa, dalawa, tatlo, ang tatay mo'y kalbo* (pronounce phonetically to catch the rhythm)—which translates into English as "one two three, your dad is bald."

Here are some fresh examples of the Pinoy Haiku, beginning with one written by Barbara Jane Reyes for Philippine Independence Day:

land
of the
mo(u)rning, i toast.

Barbara deftly conflates the reference of "land of the morning" from the Philippine national anthem with the wine theme of this WINEPOETICS blog. Relatedly, Patrick Rosal offers:

NYC Pinoy Blues or The Ay Naku Haiku

God-
damn—same
shit/different dog

Meanwhile, Leny M. Strobel and Oscar Penaranda's contributions reflect both the events over a century ago as well as the current times (the U.S. had just invaded Iraq)—befitting their shared status as scholars/teachers as well as poets:

Freedom
Is Cheap
When You're Bushed
--Leny M. Strobel

Power
Drippingly exudes

And always stains
--*Oscar Penaranda*

Here's two riffed off by Oliver de la Paz while he was doing laundry:

Keats
writes darkly.
Birds trill unseen.

Watches
around wrists
make teeth marks.

In these works, what's evident to me is that the charge associated with the haiku remains in the Pinoy form with the type of paradox that one might find in the Filipino *bagoong*—a pungent fish sauce enjoyed by Filipinos but, ahem, misunderstood by non-Filipinos. Thus, does Catalina Cariaga also offer:

onion
just eaten;
smell my breath

*****

Most of the Pinoy "haiku" (scare quotes deliberate) came from writers who belonged to Flips, a listserve of either Filipino writers or anyone interested in Filipino Literature that was co-founded by poets Nick Carbo and Vince Gotera. While my compadres and comadres happily sent me what Vince called these "Stairstep Tercets," my project also ended up eliciting a discussion on the implications of *Naming*—and how I was approaching it by using the phrase "Pinoy Haiku." Vince asked:

> Appropriating the "haiku" name has all sorts of prosodic and postcolonial problems (by which I mean the WWII "colonizing" of the Philippines by Japan, among other things). Am I being overly serious here? When you say Kerouac refers to "American haiku" not having more than three words per line, I think he might have been reacting to Allen Ginsberg's "American sentence" which has 17 syllables per line. I guess my concern about calling it a "Pinoy haiku" is that readers could say "Hey, Pinoys can't even get the haiku right!" They won't always have the Kerouac quote to guide them. Besides, why must we

> always be doing things in reaction to the term "American"? An interesting parallel poetic-form-naming might be Baraka's "low coup" form (the diametrical opposite of "high coup" / haiku). Maybe the Pinoy version could be the "hay (na)ku"?

"Hay naku" is a common Filipino expression covering a variety of contexts—like the word "Oh."

Another poet had suggested that I also rename the project because the traditional haiku form should be respected. Well, yes and no. As I told that poet—I also think that, in Poetry, rules are sometimes made to be broken.

And, I initially wasn't moved either by Vince's notion as regards Japan "colonizing" the Philippines during WWII. If anything, I thought that were I to move down that line of thinking (which I hadn't been), I didn't mind subverting the Japanese haiku form specifically because I thought of it as *talking back* against Japanese imperialism. But, on closer consideration, I realized that the perspective could work both ways...and that using the "haiku" reference also could imply a continuation of "colonial mentality."

Catalina "Catie" Cariaga also appreciated Vince's comments:

> Hey Vince, I like "hay(na)ku." That's the spirit! Like halo-halo. There's a chapter in Vicente Rafael's *Contracting Colonializm* about that guy Pin Pin who translated the Spanish grammar book into the Filipino vernacular—which ended taking all types of forms, songs, explanations and translations—perhaps to SUBVERT the very project he was assigned to "translate." I read Rafael's comments very seriously. Pin Pin used combinations of long languid fluid lines and short syllabic bursts. We have those kinds of macro and micro-rhythms in our F(P)ilipino American repertoire. Like halo-halo.

Vicente's observations, indeed, should be read by many. But, with all due respect to Vicente, I also found Catie's reply most persuasive due to the reference to halo-halo: an incredibly yummy-licious Filipino dessert of shaved ice, coconut shavings, bits of fruit jello and tropical fruits like jackfruit, banana, ...I'ma getting hungry....

Anyway, I bowed to Vince's wisdom (he is, after all, older than I am; wink here at Vince) and renamed the form "HAY(NA)KU"

*****

Since the birth of hay(na)ku, there has been a hay(na)ku contest judged by Barbara Jane Reyes which was quite popular in the internet's poetry blogland; the hay(na)ku form was taught by Junichi P. Semitsu, then Director of "June Jordan's Poetry for the People" program at the African American Studies Department at U.C. Berkeley; and many other poets—non-Filipino as well as Filipino—have picked up the form to write it as I originally conceived as well as to offer variations.

Maya Mason Fink, the 11-year-old daughter of poet Thomas Fink, concocted a variation whereby the first line has one word of one letter, the second line two words of two letters each, the third line three words of three letters each, and so on—as far as the poet wishes to take it. "The Mayan Hay(na)ku" points to one of the hay(na)ku's possibilities as an attractive tool for introducing poems to youngsters.

Kari Kokko introduced a "moving hay(na)ku" via the internet whereby, through the wonders of HTML, the lines move across the screen. Thomas Fink, a painter as well as a poet, completed a painting series that presents his visual manifestation of the hay(na)ku. His black-and-white painting "Hay(na)ku 9 (2005)" (20" X 16", acrylic on canvas) is shown on the next page.

Other hay(na)ku variations include the "Ducktail Hay(na)ku" whose ducktail references a hairstyle that shows a thin strand of hair trailing down from an otherwise shortly-cropped hair cut; this version features the three-line stanza, followed by another one-line stanza of any length. Another variation is the "Reverse Hay(na)ku" whereby the numbering of words per line is 3, 2 and 1, respectively, versus 1, 2 and 3. Wales-resident Ivy Alvarez concocted the "worm hay(na)ku using letters that don't have tops [b, d, f, h, i, j, k, l, t] nor tails [g, j, p, q and y]. The **worms** of a c e m n o r s u v w x z." At the time of writing this essay, Scott Glassman is introducing the "abecedarian hay(na)ku" sequence where each word begins with each succeeding letter of the English alphabet.

One of the most effective variations has been the hay(na)ku sequence, as epitomized in the works of Kirsten Kaschock, Sheila Murphy, harry k.stammer, Tom Beckett, Ernesto Priego and many other poets. Some of these sequences are included in this anthology. Others, as the hay(na)ku continues to develop and spread as a poetic form, have been written since submissions and considerations closed, and have appeared elsewhere.

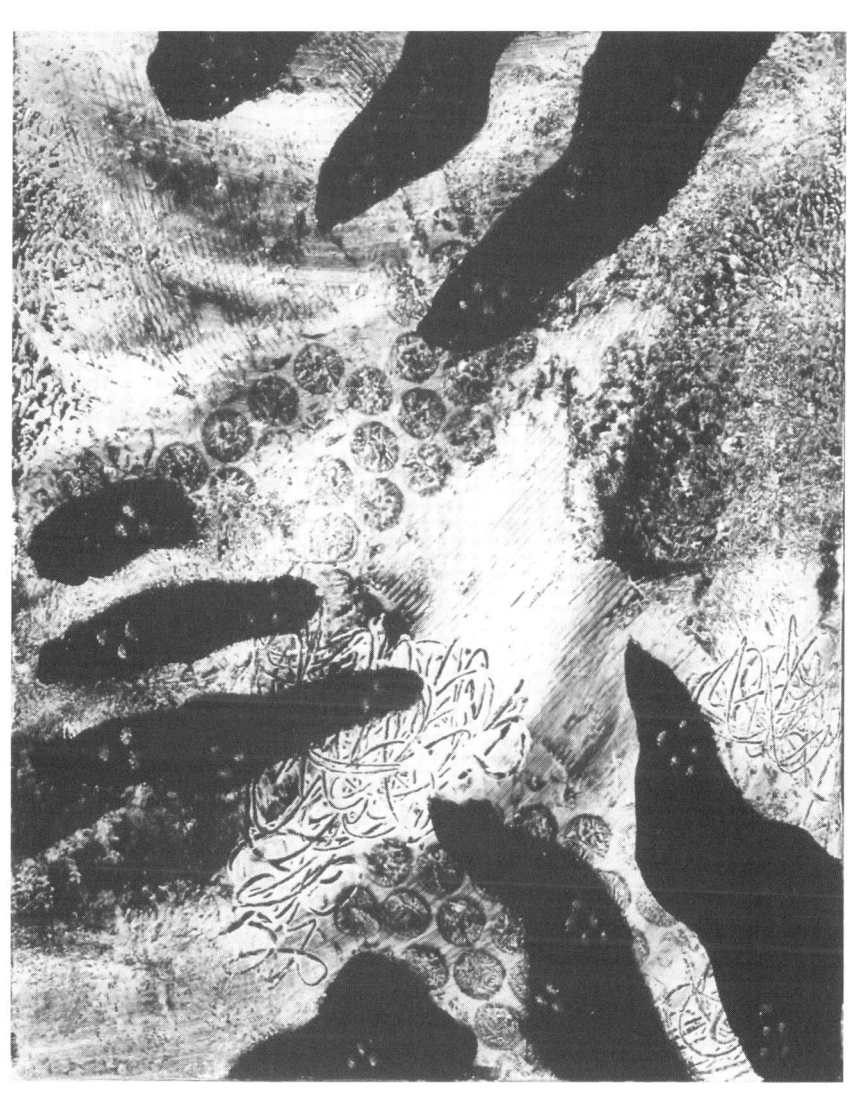

Thomas Fink: Hay(na)ku 9
2005. Acrylic on canvas, 20" X 16". Collection of the artist.
(Photo by Molly Mason)

As one can see by the history of the hay(na)ku, it is a community-based poetic form which fits my own thoughts on the poem as a space for engagement. "Community" is a word laden with much baggage -- both good and bad. I, too, have a conflicted reaction to the word. But I have to say that some of my favorite poetic projects are those where I consciously am building towards a community -- through both poetic form and content. Why? Because I think a poem doesn't fully mature without a particular community called reader(s). Poetry is (inherently) social.

*****

Since the initial response by Filipino poets to the hay(na)ku, many—if not most—hay(na)ku have been written by non-Filipinos. This is certainly a fine result since Poetry is not (or need not be) ethnic-specific. But I'm also glad that non-Filipinos have taken up this form because I consider the hay(na)ku—as I've stated on its official "Hay(na)ku Blog" (http://eileentabios.blogspot.com)—to be both a Filipino as well as Diasporic Poetic.

In the diaspora, the Filipino meets many influences and what would be the point of denying such? Given that the diaspora has existed throughout Filipino history, to call something "Filipino," in my view, is not the same as hearkening back only to so-called "indigenous" Filipino traits. I agree with Filipino poet Eric Gamalinda when he observes, "The history of the Philippines is the history of the world."

****

Ironically, I actually feel myself mostly mediocre at the hay(na)ku. I've written just a few as of the time of preparing this anthology, such as this while potty-training my puppy Achilles:

HERE WE GO AGAIN
"by" Achilles

"Go
Potty!" Mama
exhorts. Sigh. Poop.

But I also think it's appropriate that I, presumably the hay(na)ku's "inventor," may be mediocre at this form. I think this logical because I've long felt that Poetry ultimately transcends the poet's autobiography. Even when the narrative offers up elements of my own life, I consider the poem a space of engagement with others, with the results nothing I can either predict or control. In this sense, the hay(na)ku very much retains my person-hood, even as its outcomes are based on others.

For the hay(na)ku, as with any of my poems, all I can do is offer my hand and hope that someone ultimately will grasp it. For the hay(na)ku, I feel as if the entire universe wreathed itself about that writing hand. Thank you, All.

July 31, 2005
St. Helena, California

NOTES ON THE HAY(NA)KU FROM CONTRIBUTORS

It is a beautiful glass container for holding the present moment: spare and elegant, it also has an incredible capacity for breadth. The hay(na)ku form is a wonderful and witty evolution that triggers inventiveness in those who use it. **Ivy Alvarez**

Hay(na)ku is such a seductive form that I've found myself rather obsessively viewing the world through its six-word frame. It's become a problem for me. The problem isn't the form. The problem is my obsessiveness. **Tom Beckett**

I had never before heard of the hay(na)ku form. So what first attracted me to this project was experimenting with something new. While trying to write some poems in the form, I noticed that hay(na)ku reads with a breathability that other forms lack -- including the tightly coiled haiku -- but it also has its pitfalls. How exactly do you go about codifying experience into such a strict pulse? How do you give life to a subject without short-changing it? There's a disjunction -- the form is hard to write, but easy to read, quite musical. It's a fascinating puzzle. What's left out means as much as what stays in. There are little shadows that follow the poems to their ends, scattering stones in the shallows of syntax. Reading one poem, you're hearing a second poem whispered into your ear, soft as a misremembered dream. I wonder how deep these caverns go, these poems seem to say. Better bring a light. **Michael Chmielecki**

We are pattern-seekers and form-makers: we cannot escape form. Even a depiction of chaos will be, in some fundamental way, formal. Indeed, chaos is simply the unfiltered and the uncategorized. As soon as I call this bit "this," and that bit "that," I have performed an act of creation. We cannot choose to be formal; we can only choose how heavily we lean into it. Seeking patterns and making forms is simply our minds in the work of comprehension. Cognition is a winnowing, a series of choices that constrain. But constraints do not limit us; they free us. We sit down to write a poem: where to start, and where to go from there? Instead of all the cosmos, an endless wordhoard to intimidate and overwhelm us, we merely need something that rhymes with "now", or three more syllables, or only six words.

I have been attracted to the Hay(na)ku form recently because the constraint (three lines of six words: 1-2-3 or 3-2-1) sits so lightly on the composition process. I may have half-formed ideas, or notes, or single words lying around, and no other place to put them. Thinking of five more words to go with these fugitives, or reworking a phrase to bring it down to the count, is a playful and surprisingly friendly way of working. It's almost like not working at all. And yet, like all miniaturist forms, it is challenging in a way that long, discursive works are not. As Pascal quipped, "I would have written a shorter letter, but I didn't have time." **Nicholas Downing**

Finding a new form to play with is like putting on pajamas when they are fresh out of the dryer. **Jilly Dybka**

I began writing hay(na)kus because they were the new, fun thing to do. I soon found that this form was more than a trend; it functioned to build community amongst writers who may not have previously had common ground on which to converse. I find this form accessible in terms of its simplicity, its playfulness, and because hay(na)kus are (deceptively) easy to dash off. This being said, I also find that hay(na)kus are difficult to get "right." With such limited space, the hay(na)ku forces you to value (and evaluate) every word. This form also asks you to question or observe the appearance of the poem on the page. What are the implications of beginning with a single word? What happens when you flip the form and the poem whittles itself down from three words on a line to a single word as the last line? I find the drastic differentiation of the line length to be an important component of this form. There would be something unsatisfying, for me, about writing in 2/2/2. Part of the force of the form is the (surprisingly) dramatic difference between the isolation of a single word on a line contrasted by a slightly longer arrangements of words. **Monica Fauble**

I appreciate the hay(na)ku's encouragement of compression, its subtly expansive quality, and the gentle subversiveness of its Filipina-American origins. **Thomas Fink**

i like new forms & try any i hear about. hay(na)ku is interesting both for its terseness & its being a word-count form. **Michael Helsem**

Why me? Why now?
Every word counts. That's hard to resist in The Age of Logorrhea.
The form encourages paring, discourages padding.
Lines shaped by word count rather than syllable, engendering more rhythmic variety among poems and within the poem itself.
Enjambment abound, bounds.
Poems start small, grow taller, taller, then hunkerdown, dip, curtsy, until they build toward tall at the end. I read the sea there, gentle tides. (I'm so damned land-locked right now, I read the sea just about everywhere.)

They often arrive on my tongue before I can even locate pen or paper. And if you've had the chance to read some of the poems found above, the form's not so rigid that it breeds sameness. Mark Young's hay(na)ku do not read like Joseph Garver's. **Crag Hill**

I have written most of my hay(na)ku from scratch but have also used the form to recast older material (such as 'Wet waiting arms' published in this anthology) – it has a way of revealing. I also see it as a 'thinking' form – emotional as well as intellectual thinking. By allowing a lot of space on the page it keeps things tight and loose. Hay(na)ku creates or pushes certain syntactical structures, potentially disruptive through its arbitrariness. Forms aren't games, or just games – they are ways of paying attention. The 'sound' is also important, the way hay(na)ku can build. My preference is to write hay(na)ku sequences that build on the form. Free but firm. **Jill Jones**

The first poems I ever wrote were Haiku. Spare forms, I think, concentrate the imagination. Having only recently been introduced to the hay(na)ku form, I notice that writing these six word poems/stanzas causes me to pay close attention to speaking patterns--specifically the subtle ways word placement can alter tone. **Kirsten Kaschock**

I tried to write (a note on the hay(na)ku) but bits and pieces about Asian transnational citizenships and Filipino maids kept invading, so I should probably keep writing my essays. **Rachael Kendrick**

It's a form that travels well. **Karri Kokko**

The hay(na)ku form forces the poet to slow down and consider each word individually, almost as a meditation. Whereas haiku restricts the number of syllables, hay(na)ku frees the poet to perceive each word as a complete unit. **Tucker Leiberman**

Hay(na)ku
flexibly tempered
to American speech

received sound pearls
fit (un)tutored
hearing
Sheila E. Murphy

Why I love the hay(na)ku: Because of the zip and pop of it. Because of the flame and spark of it. Like snapping a towel at someone you love. **Aimee Nezhukumatathil**

The diasporic nature of the hay(na)ku attracted me from the very beginning because it allowed me to express myself in English without being a native speaker. The apparently simple form is, in practice, very challenging, and allows for a series of singular possibilities. I feel the hay(na)ku is a form that grants a common space for poetic practice in different languages; a way of writing in English without completely obliterating one's "mothertongue". Instead of the conquest and influx that has defined English in relation to other "less powerful" languages, the hay(na)ku is open and flexible, an invitation to share different ways of thought and writing. **Ernesto Priego**

It's a fresh and crispy stanza pattern that lets the sky in while keeping a path. Looks good, sounds good. **Jay Rosevear**

I love the deceptive simplicity of the Hay(na)ku form. Anyone can come up with 6 words. But to make them resonate and to instill meaning into them is the challenge. **Jim Ryals**

Hay(na)ku is an open and limitless sky wherein birds of poetic imagination can wing freely to amuse sweet souls. **Radhey Shiam**

When I think about why I 'like' something, especially a poetry form, headaches start to form (that's why we have critics? for headaches, right?). 'Like,' rarely is a reason to action for me. And that goes for any form including hay(na)ku, which I've tried to come to without definition (by definition would defeat the purpose). hay(ka)nu, for me, is a wonderful example of a form where nothing can be said wonderfully or not wonderfully in six words, letters, numbers, etc. It's "vispo" to me, baby. That's/ syllable word/ line divided dividing. Or, as the pigeon at my window just said, "t/ha/t's." **harry k. stammer**

I find the word-based formal constraint of hay(na)ku (as opposed to a syllable or metrical foot based constraint) leads to poems that are in many ways more natural, and that, in particular, the 1-2-3 structure is a pattern that comes up continually in the course of the daily. Poetry lives and breathes in the daily, and hay(na)ku has the ability to capture profound and delightful pieces that might otherwise be missed. **Dan Waber**

This form represents for--someone who spent much of his life in Japan and "toying" with the haiku format--nothing less than the key to release from my preconceived notions of style and form. Many a time I have been forced to conform to some recipe, only to loose all passion and power to evoke with my words. The hay(na)ku had given me the freedom to return to the origins of poetry in play, play with the form and, by extension, with the words themselves. Finally, I find a pleasure in structure that I never knew existed before--precisely because this form allows me to move, to grow, to transform, and yes!--to transgress my own notions of structuring. **James A. Wren**

NOTES ON THE EDITORS

Jean Vengua was born in San Francisco, California. She teaches at U.C. Berkeley, and lives in Santa Cruz and Alameda, CA. Her work has been published in various poetry journals, including *Proliferation, Interlope, Moria, Sidereality, xStream, Fugacity #5,* and the anthologies, *Babaylan, Returning a Borrowed Tongue,* and *Going Home to a Landscape.* Her essay introduces *Behind the Blue Canvas,* a collection of short stories by Eileen Tabios. With Elizabeth H. Pisares, she is co-founder of Tulitos Press (Santa Cruz/Bloomington). She is also a writer and researcher in Filipino American studies; her essays have been published in scholarly journals including *Jouvert: a Journal of Postcolonial Studies* (North Carolina State U.), *Geopolitics of the Visual: Essays on Philippine Film Cultures* (Ateneo University Press, Philippines), *Critical Mass* (University of California)*,* and the anthology, *New Immigrant Literatures of the United State*s (Greenwood Press). Her poetry weblogs are *Okir:*(http://okir.blogspot.com), and *The Nightjar:* (http://thenightjar.blogspot.com).

Mark Young, New Zealand born & now living on the Tropic of Capricorn in Australia, has been publishing poetry for more than 45 years. His work has appeared in a large number of journals, both print & electronic, in many countries. He has published nine books. Six are his poetry, two are collaborations with Jukka-Pekka Kervinen & there is also a book about New Zealand painting. His most recent books have been *Poles Apart*, a selection of his work with Jukka-Pekka Kervinen, *The Cicerone*, an extended version of one of his Series Magritte poems & *Episodes*. He has an author's page at the New Zealand electronic poetry centre, & maintains two weblogs, pelican dreaming, & mark young's Series Magritte.

NOTES ON CONTRIBUTORS

Ivy Alvarez was born in the Philippines, raised in Australia, and currently resides in Wales. Her work is published in literary journals and anthologies around the world and online. Awarded a MacDowell Colony Fellowship in 2005, she is the author of three chapbooks: *what's wrong* (Wales: The Private Press, 2004), *catalogue: life as tableware* (Wales: The Private Press, 2004) and *Food for Humans* (Melbourne: Slow Joe Crow Press, 2002).

Tom Beckett's (Ohio, U.S.A.) blog e-x-c-h-a-n-g-e-v-a-l-u-e-s (http://willtoexchange.blogspot. com) publishes interviews with poets. He is the author of *Vanishing Points of Resemblance* (Generator Press, 2004).

Raymond T. Calbay (Philippines) is a former reporter of *The Manila Times*. He now writes feature stories for a sports magazine.

Michael Chmielecki was born in New Hampshire. He lives and reads in Los Angeles. He edits four national trade publications, and splits his free time between watching movies with his roommate and working at a friend's nightclub.

Nicholas Downing (not his real name) was born in Chicago, Illinois. He maintains a blog at newbroom.blogspot.com. He lives in northern New Jersey. His interests include the shapes of things, the origins of things, and the sounds of things. Ideas are cheap, and hold his attention only briefly, like fireworks. Having spent (or frittered) many years of his life pursuing the wandering fires deeper and deeper into the wild, at present he is a sojourner in civilized life again (where he marvels how ideas trade at inflated prices while things are often cast aside like straw dogs or christmas trees).

Jilly Dybka is working on her MFA in Creative Writing at Queens University of Charlotte. She works with computers and is married to a jazz musician.

Monica Fauble is currently a MA candidate in Poetics at the University of Maine. She blogs with Stephen Kirbach at www.hatstuck.blogspot.com

Thomas Fink is the author of three books of poetry, most recently *After Taxes* (Marsh Hawk Press, 2004) and two books of criticism, including *"A Different Sense Of Power": Problems Of Community In Late-Twentieth-Century U.S. Poetry* (Fairleigh Dickison UP, 2001). His work has appeared in *Jacket, Verse, x-Stream, Talisman, American Poetry Review, Chicago Review, Denver Quarterly, Boston*

Review, Moria, and numerous other journals. His paintings hang in various collections.

Maya Mason Fink, daughter of Thomas Fink and Molly Mason, was born in 1993. The inventor of a variation on the Hay(na)ku mentioned in Eileen Tabios' essay *The History of the Hay(na)ku* called the Mayan Hay(na)ku, she lives in Long Island, New York.

Craig Freeman lives in Houston, TX. His writing has appeared or is forthcoming in *can we have our ball back?, Diagram, 5_trope, Good Foot and Fur Eileen*. He used to go by other names, most notably Joseph Garver, but got tired.

Michael Helsem was born in Dallas in 1958. Shortly thereafter, fish fell from the sky.

Crag Hill (Idaho, U.S.A.) has been exploring the world through the prisms of verbal and visual language since his re-birth in the 1970s. Writer of numerous chapbooks and/or other interventions in print, including *SIXIXSIX* (Xexoxial Endarchy), *TRAINS SL:AY HUNS* (Generator), DICT (Xexoxial Endarchy), *ANOTHER SWITCH* (Norton Coker Press), and *YES JAMES, YES JOYCE* (Loose Gravel Press), he has also edited *SCORE* magazine, a publication exploring, seeking, the edges of writing, since 1983. His latest book, co-edited with Bob Grumman, is *WRITING TO BE SEEN*, the first major anthology of visual poetry in 30 years.

Jill Jones (Sydney, Australia) latest books are *Broken/Open* (Salt, 2005), *Fold Unfold* (Vagabond, 2005) and *Where the Sea Burns* (Picaro, 2004). She won the Kenneth Slessor Poetry Prize in 2003. She has collaborated with photographer Annette Willis on a number of projects.

Kirsten Kaschock's (Georgia, U.S.A.) first book, *Unfathoms*, is available from Slope Editions. She holds MFAs from Syracuse University in poetry and in choreography from the University of Iowa. Her poems have been published in *American Letters & Commentary, Barrow Street, The Diagram, Denver Quarterly, Volt* and elsewhere.

Rachael Kendrick (Canberra, Australia) is a 22 year old womanchild, university student and sometime poet who does her best work while checking out girls. Her favourite things include dachshunds, Vanilla Ice and wasting time on the internet. She writes poetry because she doesn't get graded on it.

Karri Kokko (b. 1955) is a Finnish poet who maintains a handful of blogs, including a poet's notebook called *Muisti|kirja*; *Poem in Reverse*, a long poem written from the bottom up; and *Blonde on Blonde*, a playground for visual poetry.

Tucker Leiberman's (Rhode Island, U.S.A.) poetry has recently appeared in the e-zines *Ariga* and *Snakeskin*. He read a haiku on the *MacNeill/Lehrer NewsHour* in 1994 after winning a student competition.

Andrew Lundwall lives in the Washington, DC metro area. His work has appeared in numerous print and electronic journals internationally including *Big Bridge, Hamilton Stone Review, xStream, Miami Sun Post's Mad Love,* and *Near South*. Lundwall was a co-founder and managing editor, with Jeannie Smith, of the literary e-journal *Poetic Inhalation*.

Sandy McIntosh's (New York, U.S.A.) poetry collections include *The After-Death History of My Mother, Between Earth And Sky, Endless Staircase, Earth Works,* and *Which Way to the Egress?* His prose includes *Firing Back, From A Chinese Kitchen,* and *The Poets In the Poets-In-The-Schools*. His poetry and essays have been published in *The New York Times, Newsday, The Nation, the Wall Street Journal, American Book Review,* and elsewhere.

Sheila E. Murphy's most recent released book publication is *Incessant Seeds* (Pavement Saw Press, 2005). Other recent books include *Proof Of Silhouettes* (Stride Press, 2004) and *Concentricity* (Pleasure Boat Studio, 2004). Her home is in Phoenix, Arizona.

David Nemeth's current whereabouts are unknown. He's on the road somewhere. Once he lived in Delaware.

Aimee Nezhukumatathil is the author of *Miracle Fruit* (Tupelo Press 2003). She is assistant professor of English at SUNY-Fredonia and has a dachshund named Villanelle.

Shin Yu Pai (Texas, U.S.A.) is the author of *Unnecessary Roughness* (xPress(ed), 2005), *Equivalence* (La Alameda Press, 2003), and *Ten Thousand Miles of Mountains and Rivers* (Third Ear Books, 1998). Two books, *Nutritional Feed* (Tupelo Press) and *Works on Paper* (Convivio Bookworks) are forthcoming.
Vincent Ponka is a writer who currently works in the film industry in Toronto, Canada.

Ernesto Priego teaches critical theory and American literature at the National Autonomous University of Mexico (known as UNAM). While he specializes in the study of comic books and other forms of visual narrative, he is also a poet, translator and curator.

Francis Raven's (Massachusetts, U.S.A.) first novel *Inverted Curvatures* will be published this fall by Spuyten Duyvil. Poems of his have been published in *Mudlark, Conundrum, Untitled, Pindeldyboz, Big Bridge, Le Petite Zine* and *can we have our ball back?* Essays and articles of his have been published in *Jacket, Clamor, In These Times, The Fulcrum Annual, Rain Taxi, Sauce,* and *Pavement Saw.*

Barbara Jane Reyes (California, U.S.A.) was born in Manila and raised in the San Francisco Bay Area. She holds a MFA from SF State University, and is the author of *Gravities of Center* (Arkipelago Books, 2003). Her work has recently been nominated for a Pushcart Prize, and has appeared or is forthcoming in *Asian Pacific American Journal, Chain, Interlope, Nocturnes Review, North American Review,* and *Tinfish.*

Jay Rosevear lives in Sydney, Australia. She maintains a blog, sky bright (http://skybright.blogspot.com). She dances with poetry.

Jim Ryals (California, U.S.A.) is a a special education attorney who woke up on December 21, 2003 and started writing poetry and fictional prose again after a 25 year hiatus. He will finish his first novel by the end of the month and will immediately start his second.

Radhey Shiam is a simple ordinary citizen of India, residing in Roorkee. Contributes articles and poems specially haiku, Tanka, Sadoka, Haynaku to Hindi, Urdu and English magazines. Author of *Song of Life* published by Bharatiya Vidya Bhavan, Mumbai

harry k stammer lives and works in Los Angeles and Santa Barbara. His poetry has been published in *sidereality, dreamvirus, xStream, Znine, blazeVOX, Moria, poetic inhalation, xPress(ed)*. He has an eponymous blog at http://harrykstammer. blog-spot. com

Eileen Tabios has released a poetry CD; four e-poetry collections; and written, edited or co-edited fourteen books of poetry, fiction and essays since 1996 when she traded Wall Street for poetry. In 2005, she released the multi-genre collection *I Take Thee, English, For My Beloved* (Marsh Hawk Press). Recipient of the Philippines' National Book Award for Poetry, the Potrero Nuevo Fund Prize, and the PEN/Oakland Josephine Miles National Literary Award, she writes the poetics blog, "The Chatelaine's Poetics" at http://chatelaine-poet.blogspot.com, while steering Meritage Press from St. Helena, CA.

Dan Waber (Pennsylvania, U.S.A.) is a poet and multimedia artist by day, and the fearless editor of Paper Kite Press by night.

David C. Whiteman was born in Ft. Worth, Texas. Graduated from the University of Texas at Arlington - English major, Writing minor. Currently pursuing a teaching career in English. An amateur writer of short fiction, screenplays, poetry and songs.

Tanya Williamson is an English Major - Minor in Creative writing. Freelance journalist for "horsey magazines" such as *Equus* and *The Chronicle of the Horse*. Won the A. C. Greene Literary Festival in 2002 for short story "Of Murder, Mayhem, and Magnolias." Lives on a small farm in rural Texas with four horses, three dogs, and three cats. Also loves to do minature oil paintings of Texas Longhorns and windmills.

James A. Wren is a former professor of Japanese language and literature, now retired because of lupus, Parkinson's Disease, and a genetic seizure disorder. "The finer arts of provocation" are at the center of most of his recent writings. Having relocated from Japan, Hawai'i and more recently California, Wren now makes his home in the Deep South, round the 'burbs of Birmingham, Alabama.

MERITAGE PRESS PROJECTS
(since 2001)

"Cold Water Flat" (2001). Signed and numbered etching by Archie Rand and John Yau. Limited edition of 37.

100 More Jokes From The Book of the Dead (2001). A monograph documenting a collaboration between Archie Rand and John Yau.

er, um (2002). A collection of ten poems by Garrett Caples and six drawings by Hu Xin. Limited edition of 75 copies. Signed and numbered by the poet.

Museum of Absences (2003). Poetry collection by Luis H. Francia. (Co-published with the University of the Philippines Press.)

Opera: Poems 1981-2001 (2003) by Barry Schwabsky.

Veins (2003). A poetry broadside by David Hess.

[ways] (2004). A poetry-art collaboration between Barry Schwabsky and Hong Seung-Hye. (Co-published with Artsonje Center, Seoul.)

The Oracular Sonnets (2004). An e-publication of a visual poetry collaboration between Mark Young and Jukka-Pekka Kervinen.

PINOY POETICS: A Collection of Autobiographical and Critical Essays on Filipino and Filipino-American Poetics (2004). Edited by Nick Carbo.

The Obedient Door (2005). Poems by Sean Tumoana Finney and drawings by Ward Schumaker.

THE FIRST HAY(NA)KU ANTHOLOGY (2005). Edited by Jean Vengua and Mark Young. (Co-published with xPress(ed), Finland.)